UNLOCKING THE SECRETS TO WEALTH AND WELL-BEING

A LIFE - TRANSFORMING GUIDE

MAYANK BISEN

BlueRose ONE.com
Stories Matter
NewDelhi • London

BLUEROSE PUBLISHERS
India | U.K.

For permissions requests or inquiries regarding this publication, please contact:

BLUEROSE PUBLISHERS
www.BlueRoseONE.com
info@bluerosepublishers.com
+91 8882 898 898
+4407342408967

ISBN: 978-93-6783-307-0

Cover design: Shubham Verma
Typesetting: Sagar

First Edition: March 2025

To my incredible family, the silent warriors who have been my bedrock, shaping me into who I am today.

Acknowledgements

I am profoundly grateful to my incredible wife, Amita Singh, whose unwavering love, strength, and support have been the cornerstone of my life and this work. Her wisdom and resilience inspire me daily and propel me to reach higher.

To my son, Ansh Singh, your bright smile and unyielding curiosity remind me of the beauty of life and the responsibility, I have to pave a better world for you. May this book serve as a guide and a source of inspiration for you as you navigate your own journey.

I dedicate my heartfelt thanks to my parents, whose values and teachings laid the foundation for everything I am today. To my father, for his steadfast guidance and quiet strength, and to my mother, for her endless love and belief in my potential. Your sacrifices have been my stepping stones.

To my extended family—brothers, sisters, and close relatives—thank you for your encouragement and for being my cheerleaders. Your presence in my life is a constant source of joy and strength.

Lastly, a special mention to all my friends and mentors who stood by me through thick and thin. Your faith in my abilities kept me going, and your insights have enriched this work immensely. To all the readers who will hold this book, thank you for sharing in this journey. Your support fuels my passion.

Preface

Writing this book has been both a challenge and a privilege, a journey of reflection and discovery that allowed me to delve into the essence of personal growth, resilience, and success. This work is a distillation of my life experiences, lessons learned, and moments cherished.

At its core, this book is a dialogue—a heartfelt conversation with you, the reader. My goal has been to craft a roadmap that navigates the intricacies of life, not just from a professional or financial perspective but as a holistic journey of the mind, body, and spirit. From building a disciplined mindset to forging meaningful relationships, from conquering fears to embracing challenges, this book serves as a guide to unlocking your fullest potential.

I hope that as you read these pages, you find not only practical strategies but also inspiration and empowerment to pursue your dreams. May this book ignite a spark within you, encouraging you to face life with courage and clarity. Remember, the journey is as important as the destination, and every step you take brings you closer to the person you aspire to be.

With gratitude and hope, I offer you this work. May it serve as a beacon of light in your journey toward a fulfilling and purposeful life.

Introduction:

Welcome to a transformative journey—one that transcends the boundaries of conventional wisdom and dives deep into the ocean of life's possibilities. In this intricate tapestry of life, where complexity and opportunity are intertwined like never before, the need for a comprehensive guide has never been more crucial. This book aims to be your compass, your lighthouse, illuminating the dark, uncharted waters of life. Whether it's finance, emotional intelligence, or mental well-being, the insights you'll gain are designed to elevate you from mere survival to absolute thriving. As you turn each page, you unlock new dimensions—unveiling secrets, debunking myths, and shedding light on the dark alleys of life you perhaps never knew existed. We'll explore not just the semantics but the soul of prosperity, the heart of well-being, and the mind of success.

Contents

Five Common Reasons You Can't Stick to Discipline and How to Fix Them

Introduction

Namaste, dear readers! Picture this chapter as a heartfelt conversation between friends, all while sipping our favourite chai. We all have big dreams—maybe it's starting a business, getting fit, or buying a new home. But how many of us actually achieve them? Often, the problem is not a lack of ambition but a lack of discipline. In this chapter, we'll delve into why discipline slips through our fingers and what we can do to hold onto it. So, make your chai and settle in; we're about to get real.

1. Your Feelings Take Over

The Problem

Feelings are like the weather—sometimes sunny and sometimes rainy. One moment you're overjoyed, perhaps your favourite cricket team just won a match, and you feel like conquering the world. Then, suddenly, something minor goes wrong, and your whole mood shifts to doom and gloom. This emotional roller-coaster can make sticking to a plan really hard.

The Solution

The first thing to understand is that feelings are natural, but they shouldn't be the driver of your life. When your mood is down, take a short break. Brew some comforting chai or coffee, take a few deep breaths, and remember your goals. Your dreams deserve more than being at the mercy of fluctuating moods. So, gather yourself and get back to the grind.

2. You're Not Serious Enough

The Problem

Imagine being on a hot summer day without an air conditioner or a fan. You're sweating, and all you can think of is a cold glass of water. When you're that thirsty, you'll search high and low to quench it. That's how your goals should feel—they should be a burning need.

The Solution

Ask yourself, "How badly do I want to reach my goal?" Your dream should be as important as that cold water on a hot day. When you make your goals non-negotiable, you'll move mountains to achieve them. You'll no longer look for excuses; you'll look for solutions.

3. You Don't Know Where to Start

The Problem

Let's be honest, saying "I don't know where to start" is an outdated excuse. We live in an age where you can find out how to do almost anything with a quick Google search.

The Solution

If you can carve out hours to watch movies or scroll through social media, you can definitely find 30 minutes to research how to achieve your dreams. You don't need an elaborate plan; you just need to start. So, make those 30 minutes count, gather information, and take your first step. The journey of a thousand miles begins with a single step, after all.

4. You Waste Time on Useless Things

The Problem

We often say, "Time flies," but the truth is, time stays; we are the ones who fly away from our responsibilities. We have the same

24 hours as everyone else, but how we spend them can make or break our dreams.

The Solution

Sit down and take a good look at your daily routine. Identify the time-wasters—maybe it's watching too much TV or endless chatting with friends. Eliminate or reduce these activities and replace them with tasks that take you closer to your goals. Remember, every minute counts.

5. You Think It's Too Tough

The Problem

When the going gets tough, many people pack their bags and leave. They think their dreams are too big to achieve. But remember, no dream is too big if you break it down into smaller, manageable tasks.

The Solution

Life will throw challenges on your way; it's inevitable. Think of these challenges as a test of how much you want to achieve your dreams. Navigate through them like you would through a crowded Indian bazaar—dodging, adjusting, but always moving forward. Your dreams are worth the bumps and hurdles, so keep going.

Conclusion

Discipline is like a muscle that grows stronger with regular exercise. This chapter has given you a workout plan to strengthen your discipline muscle. So now, the ball is in your court. You have the tools; all you need to do is use them. Remember, the journey may be long and filled with challenges, but the destination is worth it.

23 Soul-Stirring Ways to Build Your Dream Life

Introduction

Namaste, dear readers! Imagine holding a magic wand that has the power to change your life. This chapter is about that wand. Are you merely surviving instead of thriving? This is your wake-up call! Make your chai, find your most comfortable chair, and let's embark on a journey that promises to change how you live, think, and feel.

1. Start Spending Time with the Right People

The Essence:

Think about your favourite Bollywood movie—there's always a hero and a villain. Now think about your life. Are you surrounding yourself with heroes who uplift you, or villains who bring you down?

The Action:

Make a list of the 'heroes' in your life—the friends and family who genuinely wish the best for you. Commit to calling or meeting them more often. Feel your spirits lift like a kite soaring in the sky during Sankranti.

Real-Life Example:

Imagine you're stuck in a job you hate, and your friend offers to help you polish your resume and apply elsewhere. That friend is your hero—keep them close.

2. Start Facing Your Problems Head-On

The Essence:

Life will throw challenges at you, much like a bowler throwing curveballs in a cricket match. You can either duck or hit a six.

The Action:

Identify your problems and tackle them one by one. It's like knocking down pins in a game of bowling. With each problem you solve, feel the exhilaration, as if you've just won a hard-fought match.

Real-Life Example:

Finding it hard to balance work and family time? Instead of getting stressed, reevaluate your schedule. Maybe you can wake up an hour earlier to get some work done, freeing up time in the evening for family. By facing the problem head-on, you're hitting it for a six, creating a win-win situation for both your work and personal life.

3. Start Being Honest with Yourself

The Essence:

Imagine standing in front of a mirror that shows not just your face but your soul. What would you see? Would you be proud or would you look away?

The Action:

Be brutally honest with yourself. It's the first step to self-improvement. Acknowledge your faults as you would point out a stain on your shirt, with the intent to clean it. Feel the chains of denial and self-deception break, giving way to the liberating wings of self-awareness.

Real-Life Example:

Do you find yourself procrastinating often, and then complaining about lack of time? Recognize this habit and own up to it—no excuses. Once you do, take actionable steps to improve, like setting specific deadlines or using a productivity app. Transform your acknowledgement into action, and feel the satisfaction that comes from self-improvement.

4. Make Your Own Happiness a Priority

The Essence:

Have you ever noticed how the first sip of chai in the morning feels like a hug for your soul? That's what prioritizing your happiness feels like.

The Action:

Find out what your 'first sip of chai' is in life. It could be painting, cooking, or even just taking a walk. Do it without guilt. Feel the joy bubble up inside you, like the first monsoon rain after a scorching summer.

Real-Life Example:

If spending an hour in the gym makes you feel alive, don't skip it for anything. That's your happiness; that's your lifeblood.

5. Start Being Yourself, Genuinely and Proudly

The Essence:

You're like a signature dish in a family gathering—unique, irreplaceable, and the star of the show. Why blend in when you were born to stand out?

The Action:

Stop mimicking what's popular or accepted. Your uniqueness is your power. Celebrate it like you would your birthday—wholeheartedly and without reservations.

Real-Life Example:

If you love classical music in an era of electronic beats, don't hide it. Your unique taste defines you; it's your special flavour in the buffet of life.

6. Start Noticing and Living in the Present

The Essence:

Ever missed seeing a beautiful sunset because you were too busy with your phone? Life's best moments happen now, not tomorrow or yesterday.

The Action:

Make it a point to really see and feel what's happening right now. It's like enjoying each bite of your favourite food, instead of eating quickly without tasting it.

Real-Life Example:

Let's say you're at a family get-together. Everyone is laughing and talking, but your mind is stuck on work for the next day. Stop for a moment. Take a deep breath. Look around and feel the love and happiness in the room. These moments are precious; don't let them slip away.

7. Start Valuing the Lessons Your Mistakes Teach You

The Essence:

Just as spices are essential for a tasty dish, mistakes are crucial for a well-lived life. They add flavour to your journey, making it rich and memorable.

The Action:

Don't just brush off your mistakes. Analyse them like a scientist—what went wrong? What can you do differently? Each mistake is a lesson wrapped in disguise.

Real-Life Example:

Missed an important deadline at work? Instead of beating yourself up, figure out what held you back. Then make a foolproof plan to ensure it doesn't happen again.

8. Start Being More Polite to Yourself

The Essence:

How often do we berate ourselves for not being 'good enough'? If you wouldn't say it to a friend, don't say it to yourself.

The Action:

Speak to yourself with kindness and encouragement. It's like watering a plant—you need to nourish it regularly for it to grow and blossom.

Real-Life Example:

Failed to stick to your diet plan? Instead of calling yourself names, gently remind yourself that tomorrow is a new day — a new chance.

9. Start Enjoying the Things You Already Have

The Essence:

Imagine your grandmother's heirloom jewellery. It may not be as shiny as new pieces, but its value lies in its history and sentimental worth. Likewise, what you already have is priceless.

The Action:

Instead of yearning for more, take a moment to appreciate what's already yours. It's akin to finding an old family photograph and reminiscing about good times.

Real-Life Example:

Do you have a stable job, a loving family, or even a pet that adores you? These are blessings that many yearn for. Take a moment each day to appreciate them, as you would a beautiful sunrise.

10. Start Creating Your Own Happiness

The Essence:

You don't need a special occasion to wear your favourite outfit or eat your favourite food. Why wait for external factors to make you happy?

The Action:

Identify what lights up your world and make it a regular part of your life. It could be as simple as calling an old friend or watching your favourite childhood movie. Feel the happiness ignite within you, like lighting a lamp during Diwali.

Real-Life Example:

Love painting but can't find the time? Schedule a 'painting hour' every week. As you see the colours fill the canvas, feel your soul fill up with joy.

11. Start Giving Your Ideas and Dreams a Chance

The Essence:

Every great achievement started as a simple idea. Shah Rukh Khan began his journey with a mere dream, and look where he is today!

The Action:

Don't shelve your ideas and dreams as unrealistic or far-fetched. Water them like a delicate plant, and watch them grow into a lush tree of achievements.

Real-Life Example:

If you have a business idea, take the first step. It could be as simple as discussing it with a friend or as big as registering the company. Feel the rush — like standing on a podium receiving a trophy.

12. Start Believing That You're Ready for the Next Step

The Essence:

Remember the first time you rode a bicycle? You were scared but excited. The next step in your life is that bicycle, waiting for you to take control.

The Action:

Banish self-doubt and take that big leap, be it in your career, love life, or personal development. The first step is the hardest, but also the most rewarding.

Real-Life Example:

Planning to buy a home but scared of financial commitment? Do your research, consult experts, and take that step. Feel the pride swell in your chest as you turn the key to your new home for the first time.

13. Start Entering New Relationships for the Right Reasons

The Essence:

Your circle of friends should be like a well-curated playlist—each one adding a unique note to your life.

The Action:

Be selective. Nurture relationships that bring out the best in you, much like the perfect blend of masala that elevates a simple dish into a culinary delight.

Real-Life Example:

Meet someone who shares your values and uplifts your spirits. Keep them close; they're a keeper, like a comforting cup of chai on a rainy day.

14. Start Giving New People You Meet a Chance

The Essence:

Not every book is judged correctly by its cover; sometimes, the best chapters are hidden inside.

The Action:

Give people a chance to show their true colours. It's like tasting a new dish—you won't know if you like it or not until you try it.

Real-Life Example:

Your new neighbours might look reserved, but they could become your lifelong friends. Take the first step—say hello.

15. Start Competing Against an Earlier Version of Yourself

The Essence:

Your life is your story, and you're both the author and the protagonist. Make sure it's a story worth telling.

The Action:

Aim to be better today than you were yesterday. It's like updating an old recipe—the same basics, but with a new twist.

Real-Life Example:

If you managed to save a small amount last month, aim for a bit more this month. Feel the pleasure of progress, like completing a challenging trek.

16. Start Cheering for Other People's Victories

The Essence:

Remember how you felt when India won the cricket World Cup? That joy in another's victory is a beautiful emotion.

The Action:

Be the cheerleader for your friends and family. It's like clapping for a performer—it adds to the joy of the moment.

Real-Life Example:

If your friend gets a promotion, celebrate with them. Your turn will come, and their joy will double yours.

17. Start Looking for the Silver Lining in Tough Situations

The Essence:

Even the darkest clouds have a silver lining, and so do your challenges.

The Action:

In every setback, look for the hidden opportunity. It's like finding a shortcut on a long and tiring journey.

Real-Life Example:

Lost your job? Maybe it's a chance to pursue a career you're actually passionate about.

18. Start Forgiving Yourself and Others

The Essence:

Grudges are heavy burdens to carry. Lighten your load by letting go.

The Action:

Forgive and move on. It's like taking off a heavy backpack during a long walk—you'll feel instantly lighter.

Real-Life Example:

Your friend forgot your birthday? Forgive and forget. Friendship is a long-term investment, not a one-day event.

19. Start Helping Those around You

The Essence:

The joy you get from helping someone is incomparable to any other.

The Action:

Be there for others, like a sturdy umbrella in a storm.

Real-Life Example:

Seen an elderly person struggling with bags? Offer to help. The smile you get in return is priceless.

20. Start Listening to Your Own Inner Voice

The Essence:

Your intuition is your internal GPS. Trust it.

The Action:

Take time to listen to your inner voice. It's like consulting a map before a journey.

Real-Life Example:

Feeling uneasy about a decision? Listen to your gut; it usually knows what's best for you.

21. Start Being Attentive to Your Stress Level and Take Short Breaks

The Essence:

You're not a machine. Even machines need to cool down.

The Action:

Recognize when you are stressed and take short breaks. It's like pausing for a sip of water during a marathon.

Real-Life Example:

Feeling overwhelmed at work? Step out for a five-minute walk. The fresh air can refresh your mind.

22. Start Noticing the Beauty of Small Moments

The Essence:

Life isn't just about the milestones; it's also about the tiny, beautiful moments in between.

The Action:

Celebrate the small joys—a child's laugh, a beautiful flower, or a delicious meal. It's like adding sprinkles to your favourite dessert.

Real-Life Example:

Got caught in a sudden rain shower? Instead of complaining, enjoy the natural refreshment.

23. Start Accepting Things When They Are Less Than Perfect

The Essence:

Perfection is an illusion. What's real and beautiful is the flaw in the diamond, the crack in the pottery.

The Action:

Embrace imperfections—they make you human. It's like enjoying a movie even if you don't agree with every plot twist.

Real-Life Example:

So, you burnt the cake? It's the effort and love that counts, not the final product.

The Journey So Far: A Conclusion

Dear Reader,

As we wrap up this transformative guide, let's take a moment to reflect on the journey you've embarked upon. We've delved into 23 crucial ways to revamp your life, each one serving as a unique tool in your self-improvement toolbox. From building discipline to living in the present moment, these aren't just tips; they are life-changing habits.

Remember, the essence of all these points boils down to one simple yet profound truth: Your life is in your hands. Whether it's facing your problems head-on, being honest with yourself, or appreciating the present moment, every single point discussed is a stepping stone towards a more fulfilled you.

But the real magic lies not in reading these points, but in living them. It's easy to nod in agreement, but the challenge—and the reward—comes in putting these principles into action. Like planting seeds in a garden, these actions will only bear fruit if you nurture them consistently.

So, as you turn this final page, know that your journey is far from over. Think of this as a beginning, a launchpad to a life that you not only live but celebrate.

Take these lessons to heart, apply them in your daily life, and watch yourself transform. Your future self will thank you for it.

47 Sentences That Will Transform Your Financial Destiny More Than A -Year Business Degree

Introduction

Namaste Future Tycoons,

What you're about to explore is not a mere compilation of sentences but a mosaic of wisdom, carefully crafted into 47 powerful mantras. These aren't just words; they're your navigation stars in the expansive sky of wealth and influence.

1. People Buy with Emotion, Then Justify with Logic.

- Feel the Pulse: Tap into the emotional core of your customer. When you do, you unlock a commitment that extends beyond mere transactions.
- National Business Example: Royal Enfield doesn't just sell motorcycles; they sell a lifestyle, a sense of freedom and adventure. When someone buys a Bullet, they're buying an identity, which they later justify with the bike's durability and performance.

2. Sell the Transformation, not the Product.

- Feel the Pulse: Sell the journey, the transformation from the 'before' to the 'after'. You're not just offering a product; you are offering a new reality.
- National Business Example: Fair & Lovely doesn't just sell a skincare cream; they sell the promise of brighter skin and, by extension, a brighter future in society.

3. State Your Price, Then Go Silent.

- Feel the Pulse: After stating your price, let the silence speak. Give your customer the space to process the value you're offering.

- National Business Example: Real estate developers in India often let the features of their luxury apartments do the talking. Once the price is quoted, the amenities and the view take over.

4. It is Easier to Sell Relief Than Dreams.

- Feel the Pulse: Understand the pain points of your customer and offer a solution. You're not just a vendor; you're a saviour.

- National Business Example: Brands like Eureka Forbes don't just sell water purifiers; they sell the peace of mind that comes from knowing your family is drinking clean and safe water.

5. Learn Psychology, Cognitive Biases, and Body Language.

- Feel the Pulse: Unlock the power of understanding human behaviour. You're not just selling to a market; you're connecting with individuals.

- National Business Example: Successful Indian politicians like Narendra Modi understand the pulse of the people, using psychological insights to connect on a deeper level.

6. A Solid Guarantee Elevates Trust

- Feel the Pulse: A guarantee is a safety net for your customer. It's your way of saying, "You're safe with us."

- National Business Example: Flipkart's easy return and refund policies have made it one of the most trusted online shopping platforms in India.

7. Memes are Marketing Dynamite

- Feel the Pulse: Memes are the language of the digital age. They're bite-sized, easily digestible, and incredibly shareable. In a noisy marketplace, a well-timed meme can cut through the clutter like a hot knife through butter.
- National Business Example: Brands like Zomato effectively use memes to engage with their audience, transforming mundane daily experiences into moments of joy and relatability.

8. Copywriting is 80% Research, 20% Writing.

- Feel the Pulse: The pen may be mightier than the sword, but it's the thought behind the ink that counts. Before you write a single word, understand who you're writing for and what they desire.
- National Business Example: Amul's topical ad campaigns are a prime example of how understanding current events and public sentiment can create a powerful and relevant message.

9. Your Product Should Fill a Need, Not Create One.

- Feel the Pulse: Authenticity wins the race. Offer solutions to existing problems rather than manufacturing new needs.
- National Business Example: Patanjali Ayurveda tapped into the existing demand for natural and Ayurveda products, offering an alternative to the chemical-laden products in the market.

10. People Care About Benefits, Not Features.

- Feel the Pulse: It's not about what your product does; it's about how it makes life better for the person using it.
- National Business Example: Maruti Suzuki doesn't just sell cars with good fuel efficiency; they sell the peace of mind that comes with low running costs.

11. Using Pictures for Written Testimonials Makes Them More Believable.

- Feel the Pulse: A picture is worth a thousand words, and when attached to a customer testimonial, it adds a layer of credibility that words alone cannot achieve.
- National Business Example: OYO Rooms often showcases customer testimonials with photos on their website, instilling confidence in potential customers.

12. You Don't Need a High-End Laptop, a Fancy Logo, or a Degree to Start a Business.

- Feel the Pulse: The tools don't make the craftsman. All you need is an indomitable spirit, a solid idea, and the grit to see it through.
- National Business Example: Dhirubhai Ambani started Reliance Industries with just a few hundred rupees and a dream. Today, it's a multi-billion-dollar conglomerate.

13. You Become Wealthy by Becoming Valuable, Then Becoming Scarce.

- Feel the Pulse: Wealth isn't just about accumulating money; it's about accumulating value. The more indispensable you become, the more you can command your worth.

- National Business Example: Dr. Devi Shetty of Narayana Health offers affordable cardiac care and has become invaluable in a country where heart diseases are rampant. His unique skill set makes him scarce, thereby increasing his value.

14. Quantify the Timeframe of Your Offer.

- Feel the Pulse: Time is money. Make it clear how quickly your product or service will deliver results.
- National Business Example: Jio revolutionized the telecom industry by offering high-speed internet within a clearly defined timeframe, gaining millions of subscribers in a short period.

15. The Market Isn't 'Saturated,' Your Offer Just Sucks.

- Feel the Pulse: Before blaming the market, take a long, hard look at your offer. Is it compelling enough?
- National Business Example: Despite the crowded e-commerce space, companies like BigBasket found a niche by delivering groceries to the doorstep, proving the market wasn't saturated, just underserved.

16. You Can Be Terrible at Sales Calls if You Have a Great Offer.

- Feel the Pulse: A fantastic product can do the heavy lifting for you. Focus on creating an irresistible offer.
- National Business Example: Tesla cars were sold out even before production, not because of persuasive sales calls but due to the allure of the product itself.

17. There Is No Such Thing as Too High a Price, Only Too Little Value.

- Feel the Pulse: If people see the value in what you're offering, the price becomes a mere footnote.
- National Business Example: Apple products are expensive, but people see value in the brand, design, and ecosystem, making the price a secondary consideration.

18. Specific Words and Numbers Are More Believable Than Broad Ones.

- Feel the Pulse: The devil is in the details. Specificity enhances credibility.
- National Business Example: When LIC says it has a claim settlement ratio of 98.04%, it sounds far more credible than simply saying "high claim settlement ratio."

19. A Happy Customer is the Most Powerful Form of Marketing.

- Feel the Pulse: Delight your customers, and they become your brand ambassadors.
- National Business Example: Zappfresh, an online meat delivery service, focused on customer satisfaction through quality and service, turning their customers into promoters.

20. Sales is About Listening.

- Feel the Pulse: The key to a successful sale is understanding the customer's needs, which can only be achieved by listening.

- National Business Example: HDFC Bank's personalized loan offers are a result of understanding the unique needs of each customer, achieved only by listening.

21. Marketing is All About Empathy.

- Feel the Pulse: Step into your customer's shoes. Understand their pain, their dreams, their daily life, and tailor your product to fill that gap.
- National Business Example: Swiggy understood the pain of waiting for food and introduced real-time tracking, winning customer trust and empathy.

22. Use the Words 'You' and 'Your' in Your Copy.

- Feel the Pulse: Make it personal. Let your customers know you're talking to them directly.
- National Business Example: Policy Bazaar uses personalized language in their communications, making insurance selection feel like a customized experience.

23. An Average Product with Great Marketing Will Outsell a Great Product with Bad Marketing.

- Feel the Pulse: Marketing is not a cost; it's an investment. A great product deserves a great showcase.
- National Business Example: Despite many superior products in the market, Maggi Noodles leads because of its marketing strategies.

24. Charge High Prices to Deliver More Value.

- Feel the Pulse: Don't underestimate the value you provide. Charge what you're worth to deliver even more value to your clients.

- National Business Example: Despite its premium pricing, Starbucks has a loyal customer base because of the value it provides in terms of ambiance and customer service.

25. Selling a Good Product in a Bad Market is a Losing Battle.

- Feel the Pulse: A fish out of water doesn't swim. Know your market before you launch your product.
- National Business Example: Tata Nano was a good car but failed because it was targeted at a segment that didn't value the "cheapest car" tag.

26. Handle Objections in Your FAQ Section to Increase Conversions.

- Feel the Pulse: Anticipate objections and address them proactively. This not only clears doubts but also builds trust.
- National Business Example: Amazon India's detailed FAQ section addresses concerns ranging from delivery timelines to return policies, increasing customer confidence to complete a purchase.

27. Your Sales Pitch Shouldn't be Over in Two Minutes.

- Feel the Pulse: Selling isn't speed dating; it's more like a courtship. Take the time to build a relationship and showcase value.
- National Business Example: Mahindra's sales representatives take ample time to explain the features and benefits of their SUVs, converting prospective buyers into loyal customers.

28. Never Sacrifice Your Reputation for Money.

- Feel the Pulse: Reputation is currency. Once lost, it's hard to regain.
- National Business Example: Titan, a Tata company, prioritizes customer trust over quick profits, ensuring long-term success.

29. To Grow, Initially Say Yes to Many Opportunities. To Sustain Growth, Learn to Say No.

- Feel the Pulse: What got you here won't get you there. Learn the art of prioritization.
- National Business Example: Infosys initially took on various types of software projects. As they grew, they specialized and started saying no to projects outside their core competencies.

30. An Irresistible Offer = Social Proof + Scarcity + Urgency + Risk-Free Guarantee + Bonuses.

- Feel the Pulse: Create an offer that's hard to refuse by touching upon various psychological triggers.
- National Business Example: Myntra's end-of-season sales utilize all these elements, making it one of the most awaited e-commerce events in India.

31. Use a Thesaurus to Replace Boring Words with Strong Ones to Increase Conversions.

- Feel the Pulse: Words have power. Choose them wisely to make your message resounding.
- National Business Example: Paytm's tagline "Paytm Karo" uses strong, action-oriented language that encourages people to use the service.

32. The Less You Care About Making Sales, the More You Make.

- Feel the Pulse: Desperation can be sensed a mile away. Focus on offering value, and sales will follow.
- National Business Example: OnePlus focuses on creating exceptional smartphones rather than hard-selling, resulting in a strong community of loyal customers.

33. It's Okay to Fire Clients That Are a Pain.

- Feel the Pulse: Not every client is worth keeping. Some relationships cost more in stress than they bring in revenue.
- National Business Example: Zoho CEO Sridhar Vembu has been open about choosing clients that align with the company's long-term vision, even if it means parting ways with high-paying but demanding clients.

34. If You Don't Think You Can Help a Prospect, Be Honest.

- Feel the Pulse: Honesty isn't just moral; it's good business.
- National Business Example: ID Fresh Food pulled off a product from the market when they realized it wasn't meeting customer expectations, earning respect for their honesty.

35. Health, Wealth, and Relationships Will Always be Marketable.

- Feel the Pulse: These are evergreen markets. If you're in one of these industries, you're in a good place.

- National Business Example: Apollo Hospitals (Health), HDFC Mutual Fund (Wealth), and Shaadi.com (Relationships) are leaders in evergreen markets.

36. Compete on Value, Not Price.

- Feel the Pulse: Price wars are a race to the bottom. Strive to offer something so valuable that price becomes irrelevant.
- National Business Example: Despite the higher pricing, people prefer flying IndiGo over other low-cost carriers due to its punctuality and service.

37. A fifth Grader Should be Able to Understand Your Writing.

- Feel the Pulse: Complexity confuses; simplicity sells. Your message should be crystal clear.
- National Business Example: Amul's ad campaigns are straightforward yet impactful, easily understood across age groups.

38. If What You Sell is Confusing, Nobody Will Buy.

- Feel the Pulse: Confusion is the enemy of conversion. Make your product as straightforward as possible.
- National Business Example: Flipkart's user interface is designed for simplicity, making it easy for even first-time users to make a purchase.

39. Use the Same Words and Phrases as Your Target Market.

- Feel the Pulse: Speak their language, hit their pain points, and watch your conversions soar.

- National Business Example: Reliance Jio used local languages in their marketing to connect with a broader audience, contributing to its rapid growth.

40. Study Talented Fiction Writers for Engaging Stories.

- Feel the Pulse: Storytelling is an art. Learn from the masters to weave compelling narratives around your product.
- National Business Example: Storytel, an audiobook service, uses engaging storytelling techniques in its marketing to attract users.

41. Your Zero-to-Hero Story is One of Your Most Powerful Marketing Assets.

- Feel the Pulse: People love underdog stories. Share your journey authentically to inspire and attract.
- National Business Example: OYO Rooms founder Ritesh Agarwal's story from a small-town boy to a successful entrepreneur, resonates with many peoples.

42. Persuasive Writing Sounds Conversational, Not Academic.

- Feel the Pulse: Write like the way you talk. Authenticity wins over jargon every time.
- National Business Example: Chumbak's product descriptions sound like a friend talking to you, making them more engaging and persuasive.

43. People Want to See Pictures of Your Product or Service in Use.

- Feel the Pulse: Show, don't just tell. Visual proof amplifies your credibility.

- National Business Example: Zomato uses real images of dishes to let customers know exactly what they're getting, enhancing trust.

44. Don't Work with Someone for a Day if You Wouldn't Work with Them for a Year.

- Feel the Pulse: Short-term gains can lead to long-term pains. Choose your partnerships wisely.
- National Business Example: Tata Motors' partnership with Jayem Automotives was strategic and long-term, focusing on mutual growth.

45. Give Value with Zero Expectations, and You'll Get a 10x Return in the Long Run.

- Feel the Pulse: Generosity pays dividends. The more you give, the more you eventually get.
- National Business Example: BYJU'S offered free access to its learning app during the pandemic, earning goodwill that will likely convert into future sales.

46. If You Are Serious About Learning, Start Reading About 100 Mental Models.

- Feel the Pulse: Expand your mental toolkit. The broader your understanding, the better your decision-making.
- National Business Example: Udaan, a B2B trade platform, used various mental models to understand market dynamics, contributing to its rapid success.

47. People Like Elon Musk, Naval Ravikant, and Warren Buffet Extensively Use Mental Models to Make Better Decisions.

- Feel the Pulse: Learn from the leaders. Adopt their strategies for rational thinking and decision-making.
- National Business Example: Ratan Tata's investment choices often reflect a deep understanding of various mental models, contributing to his long-term success.

In Conclusion

Dear Friends and Future Leaders,

If you've read up to this point, well done! These 47 tips are not just advice, they are steps to help you do better in your business and in life.

This isn't only about earning more money. It's about making a real change in your life and in the lives of those around you. Whether you're in a small town or a big city in India, these tips work for everyone.

So, this is your guide, your roadmap to success. Read it again and again, use these tips in your own life, and see how things change for the better.

Remember, every big journey starts with a single step. You've got 47 steps here. Pick one and start walking.

Wishing you all the success and happiness you deserve.

"The Ultimate Financial Playbook: 99 Essential Lessons for a Prosperous Life"

Introduction

Welcome to this illuminating journey that promises to redefine your relationship with money and success. You're about to delve into 99 vital money lessons that are more than just tips; they are life-altering principles designed to instil a winning mindset. These are hard-earned nuggets of wisdom—some of which you might have heard but perhaps never fully grasped, and some that will be revelations, opening new horizons of understanding for you.

This isn't just a guide to managing your finances. It's a holistic approach to mastering your life through the lens of money. Money is often the most misunderstood tool in our lives. It's not just currency; it's a representation of our time, energy, and values. Understanding how to manage it wisely is akin to understanding how to lead a fulfilling and enriched life.

In the coming pages, you'll find lessons divided into five major categories: Money Mindset, Income, Spending & Saving, Investing, Relationships, and Key to Success. Each category delves deep into the core principles that govern our financial and life decisions. The lessons are embellished with real-world examples, emotional triggers, and actionable steps to make them more relatable and effective.

So, grab a notepad, keep an open mind, and prepare to jot down ideas and action plans as you go through each lesson. This isn't just a read-it-and-forget-it manual; it's your life playbook. Your transformation begins now. Shall we?

Money Mindset

- MONEY IS A GAME: Imagine you're the captain of your local cricket team. The way you strategize, the risks you take, and the team you build determine whether you win or lose. Similarly, mastering money is about understanding its rules and playing the game smartly.

- FIND PEOPLE SMARTER & RICHER THAN YOU: Think of Sachin Tendulkar and how he credited his coach for honing his skills. Surround yourself with mentors who can guide you through the complexities of the financial world.

- NEVER RELY ON YOUR JOB ALONE: Ever heard of the proverb, "Don't put all your eggs in one basket?" A single stream of income is a risky strategy. Always look for additional ways to earn.

- GOOD GRADES DON'T MAKE YOU RICH: Scoring high on an exam doesn't necessarily equip you to navigate the labyrinth of financial decisions in real life. Knowledge and action do.

- EMOTIONAL DECISIONS LOSE MONEY: An emotional investor is like a cricketer who lets anger dictate his shots. Poor choices ensue. Always keep your emotions in check.

- THE BEST THING MONEY BUYS IS YOUR FREEDOM: Imagine being able to travel wherever you want, whenever you want. That's the ultimate freedom money can buy!

- IF YOU WANT TO BE AVERAGE, FOLLOW THE CROWD: The crowd usually takes the safe, beaten path. But remember, no one ever achieved greatness by playing it safe.

- YOUR NETWORK IS YOUR NET WORTH: Who you know can be as important as what you know. Your contacts can open doors that you didn't even know existed.
- SAVING ALONE WILL NEVER MAKE YOU WEALTHY: Saving is a defensive play, like a team that only focuses on defence and forgets to score. To win, you need to go on the offense by investing wisely.
- AVOIDING FAILURE ALSO AVOIDS SUCCESS: Sachin didn't hit every ball for a six. He failed, learned, and then hit the next ball even harder. Don't shy away from calculated risks.
- BE PATIENT FOR RESULTS, BUT URGENT TO ACT: A great dish takes time to cook. Similarly, the fruits of your financial decisions will take time to manifest. But that shouldn't stop you from taking immediate actions.
- "LUCK" IS PREPARATION MEETING OPPORTUNITY: The 'lucky' people are often those who are prepared to seize opportunities when they appear. Keep honing your skills and stay alert to opportunities.
- THE RICH DON'T WORK FOR MONEY: They make their money work for them. Imagine having a team of employees who work tirelessly for you; that's what your investments should do.

- YOUR PAST MISTAKES DON'T DEFINE YOUR FUTURE: Failed in a business? Lost money in the stock market? It's okay. Every dawn brings a new opportunity to rewrite your story.
- FLASHY THINGS ONLY IMPRESS PEOPLE POORER THAN YOU: At the end of the day, the brand of your car or the size of your house doesn't define you. Your actions do.

Let's continue our deep dive into this wellspring of financial wisdom. Each point here isn't just a statement; it's a life-lesson wrapped in words. Ready for more? Here we go!

Income

- YOUR INCOME IS SIMPLY THE VALUE OF YOUR WORK: Imagine being a craftsman. The finer your craftsmanship, the higher the price it fetches. Your skills and the value you bring to the table determine your income.
- PRIORITIZE LEARNING OVER EARNING AT THE START: Think of this phase as your "training season." It's like an actor honing his skills in theatre before hitting the big screen. The more you learn, the more you'll eventually earn.
- STRIVE TO IMPROVE YOUR TIME-MONEY LEVERAGE: Would you rather catch fish with a net or a single fishing line? The more efficient your methods, the more money you'll make in less time.
- THERE IS NO TRULY PASSIVE INCOME: Even a well-oiled machine needs occasional fine-tuning. The notion of earning money while you sleep is enticing, but

remember, it requires upfront work and ongoing maintenance.

- NOT ALL SIDE HUSTLES ARE WORTH YOUR TIME: It's like picking the right stock among hundreds. Some will give high returns, and some will drain your resources. Choose wisely.
- PAID BASED ON OUTPUT > PAID BASED ON TIME: Imagine being a writer who gets paid per book sold instead of hours spent writing. The more value you deliver, the more you should earn.
- YOU ARE ONE SKILL AWAY FROM 2X INCOME: Mastering digital marketing can be that one skill that catapults your consultancy business. Never stop learning.
- BUILD MULTIPLE INCOME STREAMS, ONE AT A TIME: Like a well-balanced portfolio, diversify your income. But remember, build one stream until it's stable before moving on to the next.
- MOST COMPANIES DON'T REWARD LOYALTY: It's a harsh truth. Just like in sports, you're only as good as your last game. Always be prepared to seek new opportunities.
- NEGOTIATE YOUR SALARY: Never settle for the first offer. It's like buying a car; there's always room for negotiation.
- THE MINDSET CAN TEACH YOU ANYTHING: Open your mind, and the world becomes your classroom. The more adaptable you are, the more skills you'll acquire.

- PAY WHATEVER IT TAKES TO LEARN IMPORTANT SKILLS: Consider it an investment in yourself. The returns will be manifold.
- STUDY THE PEOPLE EARNING MORE THAN YOU: They're doing something right. Analyse, learn, and implement their strategies in your life.
- KNOW YOUR WORTH & DON'T SETTLE FOR LESS: You're a unique blend of skills and experiences. Never sell yourself short.
- BIG OPPORTUNITIES DON'T COME OFTEN, BE READY: It's like catching a once-in-a-lifetime cricket match. If you're not prepared, the opportunity will pass you by.

Fantastic! Buckle up as we delve into the maze of "Spending & Saving." This section is the lifeblood of your financial journey, laying the foundation for a prosperous future. Let's dig in!

Spending & Saving

- ALWAYS LIVE BELOW YOUR MEANS: Imagine having a bucket with a hole; the lesser water you pour in, the longer it will take to empty. Living below your means is like plugging that hole.
- LIFESTYLE CREEP KEEPS YOU IN THE RAT RACE: It's like upgrading to a faster car but still being stuck in traffic. Earning more shouldn't mean spending more on non-essentials.
- CUT THE BIG EXPENSES FIRST: Focus on the elephants in the room, like that unused gym membership or the luxury car eating into your savings.

- DON'T UNDERESTIMATE RECURRING EXPENSES: They may look small, but they add up, just like a leaking faucet slowly filling the bucket over time.
- HANG OUT WITH OTHER FRUGAL PEOPLE: Surround yourself with wise spenders; their habits will rub off on you.
- YOU CAN'T OUT-LEARN BAD SPENDING HABITS: No matter how many books you read or seminars you attend, if you don't practice what you preach, it's futile.
- SPEND MORE ON THE THINGS THAT MATTER: Invest in experiences and relationships rather than material goods. These are the treasures that enrich your life.
- RUTHLESSLY CUT SPENDING ON THINGS THAT DON'T: Be as vigilant as a hawk. If it's not adding value to your life, it has no place in your budget.
- TRACK YOUR SPENDING AND REVIEW IT REGULARLY: Knowledge is power. The more aware you are of where your money is going, the better you can control it.
- BUILD AN EMERGENCY FUND, YOU'LL NEED IT: This is your safety net. Like a spare tire, you may never need it, but you'll be thankful it's there when you do.
- DELAY PURCHASES TO STOP IMPULSE SPENDING: Give yourself time to ponder. Often, the desire to buy will pass.

- CHEAPER IS NOT ALWAYS BETTER: Quality trumps quantity. A well-made product may cost more upfront but will save you money in the long run.
- CONSIDER COST-PER-USE WHEN BUYING: It's not about how much it costs but how much use you'll get out of it. A pricey but well-used item can be a better deal than a cheap one rarely used.
- DIFFERENTIATE BETWEEN NEEDS AND WANTS: Needs are non-negotiable; wants are not. Learn to tell the difference.
- CREDIT AND DEBT MUST BE USED WISELY: Think of them as tools. Used correctly, they can build you a house; used poorly, they can bury you.

Absolutely! Now, let's sail into the world of "Investing," a realm where your money doesn't just sit; it grows, multiplies, and builds your empire. Hold tight; this is where the financial thrills are!

Investing

- INVESTING IS FUNDAMENTALLY A LONG-TERM GAME: Patience is your greatest ally. Just like a fine wine, your investments need time to mature.
- TRYING TO GET RICH QUICK GETS YOU BROKE QUICK: Gambling and investing are not the same. One could lead you down a rabbit hole, while the other guides you to treasure.
- IGNORANCE AND EMOTIONS ARE YOUR BIGGEST RISKS: Equip yourself with knowledge and keep your emotions in check. A calm sea never made a skilled sailor.

- DEFINE YOUR TIME HORIZONS BEFORE INVESTING: Have a roadmap. Know your stops. This is not a blindfolded dart game.
- INVEST ACCORDING TO YOUR RISK TOLERANCE: Everyone has a different appetite. Don't eat more than you can chew.
- FOCUS ON THE FUNDAMENTALS: It's the cornerstone of every successful investment. Ignore the noise; stick to the basics.
- RISK AND VOLATILITY ARE DIFFERENT: Risk is the possibility of losing. Volatility is the ride up and down. Understand the difference.
- INVESTING WITHOUT RESEARCH IS GAMBLING: Due diligence is your compass in this investing jungle.
- FEAR OF MISSING OUT SINKS PORTFOLIOS: Don't chase after the bus you missed. There will be another one.
- THERE IS NO PERFECT INVESTMENT: Just like there's no perfect person, but the right match can make a world of difference.
- DIVERSIFICATION IS A HEDGE AGAINST IGNORANCE: Don't put all your eggs in one basket; it's as simple as that.
- INVESTING IS NOT A COMPETITION: Your only competitor is your past-self. Beat that!

- GIVE YOURSELF ROOM FOR ERROR; YOU AREN'T PERFECT: Even Sachin Tendulkar didn't hit a century every time he batted.
- UNDERSTAND CAPITAL GAINS VS CASH FLOW: One is a sprint, and the other is a marathon. Know when to run.
- LEARN THE TAX CODES ON ASSETS IN YOUR STATE: Taxes can eat into your returns like termites into wood. Protect your investment.

Absolutely, let's keep the momentum going! Now, we're diving into the "Relationship" aspect. Trust me, money and relationships are more entangled than you think. Ready? Here we go:

Relationship

- FAMILY AFFECTS FINANCES MORE THAN ANYTHING: Your family is your first financial institution. Make sure it's a healthy one.
- YOUR REPUTATION PRECEDES YOU: It's your silent business card. A good reputation can open doors that even the best key can't.
- FIND PEOPLE STRONG IN AREAS YOU ARE WEAK: Synergy is magical. Imagine forming a dream team where everyone's a star in their role.
- MARRIAGE IS A FINANCIAL EDUCATION: It's a merger, not just of hearts but also of assets and liabilities. Choose wisely.

- GIVE YOUR CHILDREN A FINANCIAL EDUCATION: The best legacy isn't wealth; it's knowledge. Equip them to build their own empire.
- MONEY WON'T IMPRESS THE PEOPLE THAT MATTER: Authenticity is priceless; never trade it for any amount of money.
- IF YOU HANG AROUND 5 LOSERS, YOU'LL BE THE 6TH: You're the average of the five people you spend the most time with. Choose your circle with care.
- FIND GUIDANCE AND MENTORSHIP: Standing on the shoulders of giants not only gives you a better view but also teaches you how to become a giant yourself.
- APPEAL TO OTHERS' SELF-INTEREST FOR FAVORS: The best way to get what you want is to help others get what they want.
- FIRST IMPRESSIONS ARE LASTING IMPRESSIONS: You never get a second chance to make a first impression. Make it count.
- DON'T LET UNSUCCESSFUL PEOPLE DISCOURAGE YOU: Naysayers will always talk. Let your success be your response.
- MONEY DOESN'T CHANGE PEOPLE, IT REVEALS THEM: In the spotlight of wealth, true characters emerge.
- JOIN PEOPLE ON THE SAME PATH AS YOU: Together, you can conquer challenges that you couldn't face alone.

- REAL FRIENDS WILL HOLD YOU ACCOUNTABLE: True friendship isn't an echo chamber. It's an accountability circle.

Key to Success

- FORTUNE FAVORS THE BOLD: Courage isn't the absence of fear; it's acting despite it. Be audacious in your pursuits.
- TAKING ACTION BEATS ALL THE SPIRITUAL FLUFF: Visualization and positive thinking are good, but action is your golden ticket to success.
- MOTIVATION IS FLEETING, PRACTICE DISCIPLINE: Don't wait for the mood to strike. Discipline is what gets you to work when motivation has clocked out.
- RETURN ON EFFORT IS NEVER PROPORTIONAL: Sometimes, a 20% effort can bring 80% results. Know where to put your energy.
- WORKING HARDER DOESN'T MEAN YOU'LL WIN: Don't confuse activity with achievement. Smart work trumps hard work.
- SMART WORK DOES NOT REPLACE HARD WORK: However, don't think smart work is a shortcut. It's just a more efficient route.
- FINISH WHAT YOU START; SEE IT THROUGH: An unfinished masterpiece is a piece of junk. Complete your tasks.

- RESULTS SHOW HOW GOOD YOU REALLY ARE: At the end of the day, your results are your report card. Make sure you're scoring high.
- YOU ULTIMATELY GET THE LIFE YOU TOLERATE: If you settle for mediocrity, mediocrity will gladly settle for you.
- TIME IS YOUR MOST VALUABLE ASSET: Unlike money, you can't earn back time. Use it wisely.
- NETWORKING IS NOT ABOUT TAKING, IT'S GIVING: Build genuine relationships by offering value, not by asking for Favours.
- LEARN TO TAKE CRITICISM: Constructive feedback is your stepping stone to greatness.
- FAILURE IS A LESSON, NOT A VERDICT: Don't be disheartened by failures; they teach you what textbooks can't.
- THE BEST INVESTMENT IS IN YOURSELF: Always allocate resources for self-improvement.
- KEEP YOUR EGO IN CHECK: Overconfidence can lead to downfall. Always be humble.
- REPUTATION TAKES YEARS TO BUILD AND SECONDS TO DESTROY: Act with integrity, always.
- YOUR HEALTH IS YOUR TRUE WEALTH: No amount of money can replace good health.
- BE A LIFELONG LEARNER: The day you stop learning is the day you start declining.

- FOCUS IS KEY: Don't be a jack-of-all-trades and a master of none.
- SMALL HABITS LEAD TO BIG CHANGE: Consistency beats intensity every time.
- ACT, DON'T REACT: Take control of your life; don't let life control you.
- CURIOSITY DIDN'T KILL THE CAT, COMPLACENCY DID: Always be inquisitive and eager to explore new horizons.
- KNOW WHEN TO QUIT: Not everything deserves your time and effort. Learn to walk away.
- AGE IS JUST A NUMBER; MATURITY IS A CHOICE: You're never too young or old to make smart choices.
- TRUE WEALTH IS HAVING OPTIONS: The ability to choose is a luxury that money can't buy.

Conclusion

Navigating the complex landscape of personal finance and success isn't a walk in the park. It demands diligence, focus, and a proactive mindset. These 99 money lessons serve as a robust framework, a personal finance 'Bible,' if you will, designed to guide you through the intricate corridors of earning, saving, investing, and living a fulfilling life.

Remember, the true essence of wealth is not just about accumulating money but mastering the art of living a balanced life. Wealth is holistic—it touches not just your bank account but also your relationships, health, mindset, and ultimately, your legacy.

So, as you turn the page on this chapter, take a moment to internalize these lessons. Reflect on them. Act on them. Make them a part of your daily life.

The wisdom encapsulated in these 99 points has the power to not just change your financial standing but to transform your life. Now, it's your turn to take the helm and steer your ship towards the uncharted waters of limitless possibilities.

Are you ready to make these lessons your life's mantras? Your future self will thank you for it.

"Unlocking the Path to Financial Freedom: Ten Time-Tested Strategies for Wealth Building"

Introduction

Greetings, aspiring wealth builders! If you're reading this, you've already taken the first crucial step towards financial independence and a more fulfilling life. Yes, wealth-building is a journey, not a sprint, and you're about to embark on an exciting odyssey that will bring you closer to your dreams, one step at a time.

You see, building wealth isn't rocket science. In fact, it's simpler than you think. But don't mistake 'simple' for 'easy.' It requires a particular mindset, unwavering discipline, and a sound strategy. That's precisely what this guide aims to provide you with: Ten profoundly simple yet incredibly effective strategies to build your wealth.

In the forthcoming segments, you'll find each strategy elaborated with real-life examples, emotional triggers to keep you motivated, and most importantly, actionable steps to help you get started right away. So, buckle up! Your journey towards building lasting wealth starts now. Ready? Let's dive in!

Strategy 1: Diversify Your Portfolio

The Essence:

You wouldn't bet your entire life savings on a single roll of the dice, would you? The same principle applies to investments.

The Action:

Spread your investments across different asset classes—stocks, bonds, and real estate. This way, even if one sector takes a hit, the others can balance it out.

Real-Life Example:

Remember the 2008 real estate crash? Those who had diversified portfolios were the ones who weathered the storm best.

Strategy 2: Time is Your Best Ally

The Essence:

In the investment world, the early bird indeed gets the worm.

The Action:

Start investing early in life to reap the benefits of compounding. Even a small amount can grow into a fortune over time.

Real-Life Example:

Take the story of Warren Buffett. He started investing at the age of 11, and look where he is now—a testament to the power of compounding.

Strategy 3: Invest in Yourself First

The Essence:

The best investment you can make is in yourself.

The Action:

Upgrade your skills, pursue further education, or even start a side hustle. The returns on investing in yourself are immeasurable and everlasting.

Real-Life Example:

Think of personalities like Oprah Winfrey or Elon Musk. They invested in their skills and knowledge, which turned out to be their greatest assets.

Strategy 4: Be Patient

The Essence:

Patience isn't just a virtue; it's a necessity in the world of investments.

The Action:

Stick to your long-term plan and ignore the noise of market fluctuations.

Real-Life Example:

Take the case of long-term investors who held onto their Apple stocks even during its lows. Their patience paid off.

Strategy 5: Embrace Knowledge

The Essence:

Knowledge is power, especially in the realm of personal finance and investments.

The Action:

Consume books, podcasts, and online resources to continuously educate yourself about the financial world.

Real-Life Example:

Self-made millionaires like Tony Robbins attribute their success to their never-ending quest for knowledge.

Strategy 6: Look Beyond Stocks

The Essence:

Stocks aren't the only game in town.

The Action:

Consider investing in alternative options like peer-to-peer lending, index funds, and robo-advising.

Real-Life Example:

The success of platforms like Lending Club shows the potential of peer-to-peer lending as a lucrative investment.

Strategy 7: Mind the Fees

The Essence:

Costs can be the silent killer of investment returns.

The Action:

Opt for low-cost investment options like index funds or ETFs to maximize your returns.

Real-Life Example:

Jack Bogle, the founder of Vanguard, revolutionized investing with his low-cost index funds.

Strategy 8: Keep Your Emotions in Check

The Essence:

Don't let emotions dictate your investment decisions.

The Action:

Steer clear of impulsive actions driven by market volatility.

Real-Life Example:

Those who panicked and sold their stocks during the 2020 market crash missed the subsequent recovery.

Strategy 9: Eliminate High-Interest Debt

The Essence:

Debt can be a massive roadblock on your journey to wealth.

The Action:

Prioritize paying off high-interest debts like credit card balances before you dive into investing.

Real-Life Example:

Financial gurus like Dave Ramsey advocate the snowball method to tackle high-interest debts effectively.

Strategy 10: Seek Professional Guidance

The Essence:

When in doubt, seek expert advice.

The Action:

Consult a trusted financial advisor to navigate the complex landscape of investments.

Real-Life Example:

Even investment moguls like Warren Buffett consult experts to make well-informed decisions.

Conclusion

Congratulations, you've just taken a significant leap in understanding the principles that can set you on the path to financial independence. These aren't just strategies; they are your blueprint for success. Remember, building wealth is a marathon, not a sprint. The key lies in being consistent and disciplined in your approach.

These ten strategies are like the ten commandments of personal finance. Write them down, stick them on your wall, or carry them in your wallet. Let them be your guiding light as you navigate the challenging yet rewarding path to wealth.

You've got the tools, the examples, and the motivation. Now, all that's left is for you to take action. So, what are you waiting for? Your future self will thank you. Here's to your journey towards immense wealth and endless possibilities! Cheers!

Unveiling the Genius Within: A Comprehensive 90-Day Journey to Cultivating a Super-brain

Introduction

Welcome to an enthralling journey, a 90-day transformative expedition that promises to unleash the limitless potential hidden within the corridors of your brain. Imagine a life where your brain functions at its optimal level every single day, granting you enhanced focus, improved memory, and a calm, clear mind to tackle even the most complex problems. If you're committed to this vision, let's embark on this life-changing journey now.

1. Reduce Salt Intake

The Essence:

Salt is not just a flavour enhancer; it's a double-edged sword that can raise your blood pressure and, in turn, wreak havoc on the delicate blood vessels in your brain.

Your Action Plan:

Switch to herbs and spices like oregano, paprika, and garlic powder to season your food. The joy you'll feel when you realize your brain fog has lifted will make you forget all about that salt shaker.

Deep Dive:

Reduced salt intake not only benefits your brain but also contributes to overall cardiovascular health. Imagine the euphoria of living a life where you're not constantly bogged down by headaches or the mental fatigue that comes with high sodium levels.

2. Promote Healthy Gut Flora

The Essence:

Your gut isn't just responsible for digestion; it's your second brain. The neurotransmitters in your gut directly impact your mood and cognitive function.

Your Action Plan:

Fermented foods like yogurt, kefir, and sauerkraut are your allies. Include them in your daily meals to nourish your gut flora.

Deep Dive:

A healthy gut contributes to a strong immune system, heart health, brain health, improved mood, healthy sleep, and effective digestion, and it may even help prevent some cancers and autoimmune diseases. Imagine waking up with a sharp mind and a body full of energy, ready to conquer the day.

3. Challenge and Train Your Brain

The Essence:

A stagnant pond breeds mosquitoes, and a stagnant brain breeds decay. Keeping your brain active and engaged is vital for long-term health.

Your Action Plan:

Dive into activities that force you to think—like Sudoku, chess, or learning a new instrument. Feel the exhilaration as you find yourself solving problems more efficiently at work or remembering details with uncanny accuracy.

Deep Dive:

Think about the elation you'll experience when you can effortlessly recall names, places, and important dates. The empowerment you'll feel is immeasurable.

4. Monitor Blood Pressure

The Essence:

Unchecked high blood pressure is a silent destroyer that can lead to a decline in cognitive skills and even contribute to dementia.

Your Action Plan:

Regular check-ups and constant monitoring can save you from future regret.

Deep Dive:

Imagine a life without the constant fear of a stroke or cognitive decline. It's not just about adding years to your life but life to your years.

5. Follow a Mediterranean-Style Diet

The Essence:

This diet is the Holy Grail for your brain. Rich in antioxidants and healthy fats and low in sugar, it's a boon for cognitive function.

Your Action Plan:

Stock your pantry with olive oil, whole grains, and fresh produce. Enjoy the burst of flavours in each meal, knowing you're nourishing your brain with every bite.

Deep Dive:

Imagine biting into a sumptuous meal, fully aware that each ingredient is a building block for a healthier, happier you. The mental clarity you'll gain will empower you to tackle even the most complex problems with ease.

Conclusion

If you've reached this far, pat yourself on the back. You're on the verge of making the most significant investment in your life—investing in your brain. The next 90 days could be the turning point in your life, the phase where you break free from the shackles of mental lethargy and ascend towards unparalleled cognitive brilliance. So, are you ready to unleash your Super brain? The countdown begins now. Unveil the genius within!

The Pillars of Fatherhood: 20 Traits to Raise Resilient and Loving Children

Introduction

Dear Fathers and Fathers-to-Be,

The mantle of fatherhood is a sacred one, imbued with responsibilities and rewards that go beyond the mere biological connection with your child. It's a lifelong commitment to nurturing, protecting, and guiding a young life. This guide aims to delve into 20 essential traits that elevate a man from being just a father to being a great one. Here, you'll find a blend of age-old wisdom and modern-day insights, all aimed at helping you be the best father you can be.

Storytelling

Why It Matters:

Storytelling is an age-old method for imparting wisdom and values. Through tales, both real and fictional, you can teach lessons that will stay with your child for a lifetime.

Real-World Connection:

My father once told me a story about how he helped a stranded family change a flat tire in the middle of the night. This simple act of kindness taught me the importance of compassion and willingness to help others, values that I cherish to this day.

Accountability

Why It Matters:

Accountability is the cornerstone of trust. Being accountable to your family means showing up, fulfilling promises, and standing by them in times of joy and crisis.

Real-World Connection:

Whether it's attending every school recital or being there to bandage a scraped knee, the consistency in your actions will teach your children the value of reliability and trust.

Confidence

Why It Matters:

Confidence is more than just self-assurance; it's a trait that encourages the same in those around you, particularly your children.

Real-World Connection:

When you take on challenges head-on, be it at work or in fixing a leaky faucet at home, you're teaching your children that challenges are just opportunities for growth.

Discipline

Why It Matters:

Discipline is about having the mental and emotional strength to make the right choices, even when they are the hard choices.

Real-World Connection:

Whether it's adhering to a fitness regimen or being punctual, your disciplined lifestyle serves as a living lesson for your children on the importance of structure and self-control.

Presence

Why It Matters:

Being present doesn't just mean physical proximity. It means giving your undivided attention and time, showing your children that they are valued.

Real-World Connection:

Spending quality time with your children, like a dedicated "Father-Kids Day" once a month, can have a significant impact on their emotional well-being.

Patience

Why It Matters:

Patience isn't just a virtue; it's a skill that your children will learn primarily from you. The patience you exhibit helps create a peaceful home and sets the stage for open communication.

Real-World Connection:

Whether it's answering the endless 'why' questions from your curious five-year-old or enduring teenage mood swings, your patience teaches your kids the importance of calm and measured interactions.

Humility

Why It Matters:

Humility is the key to balanced success. It helps one recognize that individual achievements are collective efforts involving support and sacrifice from others.

Real-World Connection:

Volunteering at a local shelter or simply helping a neighbour in need can teach your children that success and humility can and should go hand-in-hand.

Sense of Humour

Why It Matters:

A good sense of humour can lighten most burdens and brighten any room. It teaches your children to find joy and laughter even in challenging times.

Real-World Connection:

Your willingness to laugh at yourself, to find humour in life's challenges, not only eases stress but also teaches your children the invaluable skill of finding light in the darkness.

Integrity

Why It Matters:

Integrity is doing the right thing, even when no one is watching. It's a principle that children will mimic, as children are great imitators and will often follow your moral compass.

Real-World Connection:

When you return extra change given to you mistakenly by a cashier, you're teaching your child that honesty holds a value greater than money.

Sacrifice

Why It Matters:

The sacrifices you make, both big and small, teach your children about priorities and the importance of putting loved ones ahead of personal desires or comfort.

Real-World Connection:

Skipping an important sports game to attend your child's school event shows them that family always comes first.

Consistency

Why It Matters:

Consistency in behaviour and values provides a stable and secure environment, a cornerstone for your child's healthy emotional development.

Real-World Connection:

Your steadfast adherence to family traditions, be it a Sunday family dinner or an annual camping trip, creates a sense of security and belonging for your children.

Encouraging

Why It Matters:

Encouragement is the wind beneath your child's wings. It's the force that propels them to venture into the world with confidence and a belief in their capabilities.

Real-World Connection:

Your words of encouragement during their first bicycle ride, their first public speech, or their first job interview can instil a sense of self-worth that no external validation can provide.

Serves His Wife

Why It Matters:

The relationship between parents sets the framework for your child's understanding of love, companionship, respect, and gender roles.

Real-World Connection:

When you treat your spouse with love and respect, help out with chores, or simply listen to her, you set an example of what a healthy relationship looks like.

Empathy

Why It Matters:

Empathy is the ability to understand and share the feelings of others. It's the foundation of compassion and a key to good social behaviour.

Real-World Connection:

When you show empathy towards your child's struggles—be it a difficult math problem or a schoolyard dispute—you teach them the value of understanding and emotional intelligence.

Loving

Why It Matters:

Unconditional love forms the emotional backbone of your child. It provides them with the security and self-esteem that serve as the foundation for all future relationships.

Real-World Connection:

Your hug after a bad day at school or your words of unconditional love, even when they've made a mistake, create an emotional safe haven for your child.

Protector

Why It Matters:

The innate sense of security that a father provides can often not be replicated. It's the assurance that 'everything will be okay,' which every child needs.

Real-World Connection:

Your presence at the bedside following a bad dream can go a long way in making your child feel safe and secure.

Lifelong Learner

Why It Matters:

A father who is a lifelong learner sets an example for the importance of continuous education, curiosity, and personal growth.

Real-World Connection:

Your active interest in books, courses, or even educational TV shows will encourage your children to be curious and value education.

Discernment

Why It Matters:

Discernment is the ability to judge well—to differentiate between what's right and wrong, beneficial and detrimental.

Real-World Connection:

Discussing with your children why you made specific life choices, like career moves or large purchases, helps them understand the decision-making process.

Sense of Purpose

Why It Matters:

A father with a sense of purpose is a role model who teaches his children to live with intention and direction.

Real-World Connection:

Whether it's your dedication to your career, a cause, or the family itself, seeing you live with a sense of purpose inspires your children to seek their own path in life.

Emotional Intelligence

Why It Matters:

Emotional intelligence is the ability to understand and manage your own emotions, as well as those of the people around you.

Real-World Connection:

Sharing your struggles and victories, your fears and joys, teaches your children that it's okay to be human, to be vulnerable, and to talk about their feelings.

Conclusion

Fatherhood is not a role for the faint of heart. It demands a vast array of qualities and skills, ranging from the ability to be a good storyteller to possessing emotional intelligence. It's a lifelong journey of love, sacrifice, and immense rewards. Every dad has his unique style, but these 20 traits serve as a universal guide for anyone committed to being a great father. So, dear dads, as you navigate the rewarding path of fatherhood, may these traits be your guiding stars.

Breaking the Chains of Overthinking: 8 Proven Strategies for a Calmer Mind

Introduction

Have you ever found yourself entangled in a web of thoughts so intricate that it leaves you paralyzed? Welcome to the world of overthinking—a space where your mind becomes your biggest adversary. This chapter aims to arm you with eight robust strategies to liberate yourself from the clutches of overthinking and embrace a more fulfilling, peaceful life.

1. The Problem is Rarely the Problem: An In-Depth Analysis

Believe it or not, the real problem isn't what you're obsessing over. It's the energy and time you're wasting, feeding the monster of overthinking. More often than not, the issue at hand constitutes only 1% of the harm; the remaining 99% is self-inflicted through catastrophic thinking.

2. Say No to Self-Rejection

In a world where social approval dictates our actions, it's easy to slide into the pitfall of self-rejection. Whether it's a job application or a simple email, don't let your thoughts sabotage your actions. Remember, you miss 100% of the shots you don't take.

3. The Power of Silence and Time

When your thoughts are spiralling out of control, the remedy isn't more thought—its silence. This strategy isn't about avoidance; it's about providing yourself the space to breathe and reset.

4. Ask Yourself an Important Question

When you feel trapped in a loop of overthinking, challenge yourself: "Is there anything I can do right now to change the situation?" If yes, act on it. If no, find peace in letting go. Your mental health is too precious for unnecessary turmoil.

5. Embrace the Power of Now

The past is a place of reference, not residence. The future is a canvas, not a cage. What you have is the present moment. Use it wisely to create a life worth living.

6. Fact-Check Your Thoughts

In emotionally charged situations, your thoughts can deceive you. Before accepting these thoughts as truth, put them under the microscope. Ask yourself, "Is this a fact or a feeling?"

7. Acceptance is the Key to Peace

Remember, what you resist persists. Acceptance doesn't mean resignation; it means understanding that you can't control everything. Peace arrives the moment you accept the things you cannot change.

8. True Health Starts in Your Mind

No amount of organic food or yoga can substitute for mental well-being. True health is a peaceful mind, and that's where your focus should be.

Takeaways

Overthinking is a battle fought primarily in the mind, and it's a battle you can win. Equip yourself with these eight strategies, practice them regularly, and watch as the fog of overthinking lifts, revealing a more focused, peaceful, and joyous you.

"Crafting Your Future: A Year to Transformation"

Introduction to the Section

In this part of our journey together, we turn the spotlight on personal evolution. This isn't just another chapter in the book of your life; it's a toolkit designed for real change. Here, you'll find practical tips that serve as stepping stones to a more fulfilling future.

Tip 1: Conduct a Life Audit

It's time for a reality check on your life's path. Assess the key areas: your health, finances, personal development, relationships, career, self-care, your home, and leisure. Pinpoint where a positive tweak can lead to a significant leap forward in your life.

Tip 2: Shift Your Mindset

The lens through which you view the world shapes your reality. Flip the script from feeling like a victim to being in control. Embrace the power of positive thinking and start acting on it.

Tip 3: Sketch Out Your Vision

Craft a vision that goes beyond daily tasks and addresses your ultimate aspirations. This vision is your north star, guiding you through life's voyage with purpose and passion.

Tip 4: Commit to Daily Growth

With your vision as your compass, forge ahead daily. Personal growth is a daily endeavour, much like nurturing a garden, where consistent care yields the most beautiful blooms.

Tip 5: Design Your Success Environment

Your environment should mirror the life you aspire to. Surround yourself with go-getters and achievers, and you'll find the road to success less daunting.

Tip 6: Expand Your Skill Set

Investing time in learning new skills can be the game-changer you need. Immerse yourself in knowledge and practice, and watch as new doors of opportunity swing open.

Tip 7: Sidestep the Negative

Distractions and detractors will come, but staying focused on your goals is paramount. Keep your gaze fixed on what matters most—your dreams and ambitions.

Conclusion of the Section

"Crafting Your Future: A Year to Transformation" is more than just a collection of advice; it's an actionable plan for the year ahead. Each tip is a catalyst for change, pushing you closer to the life you've envisioned. Embrace these principles, apply them diligently, and watch as the ordinary transforms into the extraordinary. Let's continue to turn the pages of this book not just with our hands but with our actions, making every chapter count.

Pathways to Transformation: Changing Your Life One Step at a Time

Introduction

In "Pathways to Transformation: Changing Your Life One Step at a Time," we embark on a journey to explore the essence of personal change and growth. This guide is for anyone standing at the crossroads, seeking a direction towards a more fulfilling life. With simple wisdom and actionable insights, we dive into the heart of transformation, illustrating how small shifts can lead to profound changes. It's a narrative that resonates with the dreams and aspirations of every individual looking to carve out a better version of themselves in this vibrant tapestry of life.

Overview of Transformational Steps

- Passion as Your Compass: Imagine waking up every day excited to work on something you deeply care about—this is what life feels like when your work aligns with your passion. It's like choosing a career in music because every note makes your heart sing, rather than settling for a job that feels off-key.

- Resilience in the Face of Adversity: Think of the countless stories of successful people who saw failure not as a roadblock but as a stepping stone. It's the courage to continue, like a batsman who keeps playing despite a series of bad innings, knowing a century is just around the corner.

- Daring to Dream Big: Envision your dreams as the seeds of your future. Plant them with care, water them with ambition, and watch as they grow into realities that once seemed as distant as the stars.
- Opportunities in Difficulties: Every challenge carries within it the seeds of opportunity. It's like the monsoon rains that may disrupt life but also bring the promise of fertile fields and bountiful harvests.
- Authoring Your Destiny: The power to shape your future lies within you. It's about making choices that reflect who you aspire to be, like a sculptor chiselling away at a block of marble to reveal the masterpiece within.
- The Foundation of Self-Belief: Trusting in your ability to succeed is half the battle won. It's like a student who believes they can ace an exam, dedicating hours to study because they know their effort will pay off.
- The First Step Forward: Transformation begins with a single step. Even the grandest journey starts with the courage to move forward, like taking the first step onto a stage before a performance.
- Breaking Free from Doubt: Overcoming self-doubt is essential. Imagine the freedom of a bird that decides it's time to fly, leaving the safety of its nest behind.
- The Power of Initiative: Action is the fuel of progress. It's about not waiting for the perfect moment but making the moment perfect by daring to begin.
- Crafting Happiness: Happiness is a personal creation. It's found in moments of gratitude, in the joy of helping others, and in the peace of a quiet moment alone.

- Creating Your Future: Your future isn't a matter of chance; it's a canvas waiting for your brush. Each goal you set is a stroke of colour that brings your picture of tomorrow to life.
- Challenging Your Limits: The only real barriers are those you set for yourself. Imagine what you could achieve if every "I can't" became an "I'll try."
- Risk-Taking for Growth: Embrace the unknown with open arms. It's about seeing risks as adventures, much like setting sail to explore uncharted waters.
- Responding with Positivity: Life is defined not by what happens to you but by how you respond. Choose positivity, like the sun breaking through the clouds after a storm.
- Learn from Every Failure: Every setback is a lesson in disguise. It's about rising each time you fall, like a phoenix reborn from ashes, ready to soar once again.

Conclusion

"Pathways to Transformation: Changing Your Life One Step at a Time" is more than a guide; it's a companion on your journey to self-discovery and personal growth. Each chapter in this book mirrors the steps you take in life, encouraging you to move forward with courage, hope, and unwavering determination. As you turn these pages, remember that transformation is within reach, one step, one decision, and one day at a time. Here's to the journey ahead—may it lead you to the life you've always dreamed of.

Thank you for joining us on this transformative adventure.

The Financial Wisdom I Wish I'd Known in My 20s: Lessons Learned in My 30s

Introduction

Your 20s are a crucial period for financial decision-making, yet most people enter this phase with little to no financial literacy. The lack of early financial education can often lead to poor choices that echo throughout life. However, your 30s can be a time of financial awakening, full of lessons that can set you on the path to prosperity. This chapter aims to bridge that gap, offering the financial insights I wish someone had shared with me a decade ago.

Buy Assets: The Golden Ticket to Wealth

Owning assets is non-negotiable if you aim for financial independence. Wealthy individuals commonly invest in a mix of assets like index funds, real estate, or their businesses. Your portfolio might not be diverse initially, but remember, Rome wasn't built in a day.

Opt for Low-Cost Index Funds: Smart and Simple

Index funds offer a low-cost, effective way to get into the stock market. Examples like Nippon India Index S&P BSE Sensex, HDFC Index S&P BSE Sensex Fund, and Tata S&P BSE Sensex Index Direct serve as solid options. (SEBI Disclaimer: This is just for reference.)

Avoid Picking Individual Stocks: The Risky Gamble

Picking individual stocks is akin to betting on a horse race without understanding the track or the horses. Research indicates that broad market investments usually outperform individual stock selections.

Know Your Risk Tolerance: The Emotional Quotient of Investing

Your risk tolerance can only be truly understood when you are fully invested. Consider starting with a demo account to gauge your comfort level with market volatility without risking your savings.

Participate in Your Employer's Retirement Plan: A Guided Path

If your employer offers a retirement savings match, that's free money on the table! As of mid-2022, around 294,000 individuals became 401(k) millionaires by wisely investing in their employer-sponsored plans.

Consider Alternative Retirement Accounts: Plan B

Not all employers offer retirement benefits. In that case, look into Individual Retirement Accounts (IRAs), which offer similar tax advantages.

Set Financial Goals: Your Financial Roadmap

Just as you wouldn't embark on a road trip without a map, you shouldn't approach your finances aimlessly. Whether you're saving for a down payment or planning your retirement, define your financial goals clearly.

Establish an Emergency Fund: Your Financial Safety Net

Life is unpredictable. An emergency fund can serve as your financial cushion for those 'rainy days.' A good rule of thumb is to have at least three to six months' worth of living expenses set aside.

Stay Out of Bad Debt: The Financial Quicksand

Debt can be a double-edged sword. While some debt can be useful for building credit or making important purchases, irresponsible use of credit cards can lead you into a financial abyss.

Automate Your Investments: Set It and Forget It

Automating your investments ensures consistency, which is vital when you're young. It not only saves time but also allows you to track your financial progress more efficiently.

Takeaways

- Asset ownership is the cornerstone of wealth-building.
- Low-cost index funds offer a less risky entry into the stock market.
- Know your risk tolerance to make more informed investment decisions.
- Employer-sponsored retirement plans are a goldmine; don't miss out.
- Always have a financial safety net in the form of an emergency fund.
- Debt, if not managed wisely, can be your downfall.
- Automating investments keeps you disciplined and on track.

By learning these financial lessons in your 30s—or even earlier—you can set yourself up for a more secure and prosperous future. After all, it's never too late to take control of your financial destiny.

Empowering Tomorrow's Millionaires: A Comprehensive Guide to Financial Education for Kids

Introduction:

The Gift of Financial Wisdom for the Next Generation

In a world teeming with financial complexities and uncertainties, one of the most valuable gifts we can offer our children is the wisdom of money management. Money, often considered a taboo topic in many households, is an indispensable part of life that children will inevitably have to navigate. The earlier they grasp these fundamental concepts, the better equipped they will be to make sound financial decisions that can influence their quality of life. This guide aims to provide parents with effective tools and conversation starters to impart financial literacy to their children. We'll explore 11 fundamental money rules, the difference between being cheap and frugal, 20 creative ways to teach kids about saving, and 12 essential money conversations you should be having with your children.

11 Money Rules for Kids: The Financial Commandments

1. Prioritize Needs Over Wants

Children need to understand the difference between 'needs' and 'wants'. Make this rule relatable by using their weekly allowance as an example. If they spend all their allowance on candy, they won't have enough left for a school project.

2. Practice Delayed Gratification

Use the classic "marshmallow test" to teach them the importance of waiting for a better reward.

3. Give Back and Count Your Blessings

Charity jars can be a good starting point. Every week, ask them to put a small amount into the jar and donate it at the end of the month.

4. Mistakes Are Good, Learn from Them

Every mistake is a learning opportunity. If your child spends on a toy that breaks easily, use this incident to discuss the importance of quality over quantity.

5. Have Fun and Enjoy Your Money Responsibly

Teach them budgeting by planning a fun day out. Let them decide how to spend a given budget on activities and snacks.

6. Save Before Spending

Open a savings account for them. Encourage them to deposit a certain percentage of their allowance or gift money into this account.

7. Don't Prioritize Money Over Health, Family, etc.

Use examples to show them that some things in life are priceless. For example, the value of a family dinner cannot be compared to an extra hour of overtime work.

8. Investing Creates More Wealth than Just Saving

Start a mock stock investment game with them. Track real stocks and discuss why some go up or down.

9. Abundance Mindset

Share stories of successful people who started with little but had a positive outlook and eventually succeeded.

10. Never Stop Learning & Keep Increasing Earning Power

Use real-life examples of people who invested in education and skills to grow in their careers.

11. Create Passive Income Streams

Discuss the concept of passive income. Use relatable examples like earning from a lemonade stand or selling crafts online.

Teach Kids about:

Cheap vs. Frugal: Understanding Value Over Price "The Psychology of Spending"

Cheap: Only Cares About Price

Cheap people often go for the lowest price tag without considering the value or quality of the item. This can lead to short-term gains but long-term losses when the cheaply bought item breaks down quickly.

Frugal: Focuses on Value More Than Price

Frugal people, on the other hand, consider the overall value of a purchase. They factor in the quality, longevity, and usefulness of an item, even if it means spending a little more upfront.

Teaching Moment:

Use real-world examples to illustrate the difference. For example, buying a quality pair of shoes that last years is more frugal than purchasing cheap shoes that need to be replaced every few months.

18 Ways to Teach Kids to Save

1. Price Match

Teach them to compare prices across stores to get the best deal.

2. Borrow Items

Before making a purchase, consider if the item can be borrowed or rented.

3. Shop Off-Season

Buy winter clothes in the summer and vice versa to get items at a discount.

4. Use Points Cards

Explain how loyalty cards can lead to savings and even free items.

5. Buy Used vs. New

Discuss the value in buying certain items second-hand.

6. Ask for a Rain Check

If a sale item is out of stock, teach them to ask for a rain check.

7. Stick to the Shopping List

Plan out shopping trips and stick to the list to avoid impulse buys.

8. Calculate Work Hours for Purchase

Explain how many hours they would need to work to afford a particular item.

9. Use Coupons and Discounts

Teach them to look for coupons in newspapers or online.

10. Have Fun without Spending

Plan activities that require little to no money.

11. Price Compare

Use online tools to compare prices before making a purchase.

12. Purchase in Bulk

Buying in bulk can lead to significant savings over time.

13. Wait 48 Hours before Buying

Implement a waiting period to avoid impulse buying.

14. Use Work Perk Programs

If applicable, show them how to use your work benefits to save money.

15. Determine Needs vs. Wants

Teach them to ask themselves if the item is a need or a want.

16. Sign Up for Promotional Emails

Use a separate email to receive promotional discounts and offers.

17. Join Customer Programs

Explain the benefits of being a loyal customer.

18. Consider Opportunity Cost

Teach them to think about what else could be done with the money.

11 Money Conversation Starters with Kids

1. Is a Cell Phone a Need?

Discuss the difference between "needs" and "wants," and where a cell phone falls in those categories.

2. What Are You Grateful For?

Encourage kids to appreciate what they have, fostering a mindset of abundance over scarcity.

3. Can We Live Without Money?

Explore the concept of money's role in society and whether it's possible to live without it.

4. Why Is It Important to Save Money?

Talk about the benefits of saving, such as preparedness for emergencies or future investments.

5. What's More Important Than Money?

Discuss values like health, relationships, and happiness, which can't be bought with money.

6. Why Is It Important to Donate Money?

Explain the concept of philanthropy and the importance of giving back to the community.

7. Is Everyone Who Has a Big Mansion Rich?

Teach them that wealth is not always as it appears; it can be tied up in assets or even debt.

8. Why Do We Need to Shred Important Documents?

Discuss the importance of protecting personal information to prevent identity theft.

9. What Would Happen if We Didn't Pay Our Electricity Bill?

Use this question to introduce the concept of bills, budgeting, and the consequences of not meeting financial obligations.

10. How Much Money Do You Want to Earn One Day? Why?

Encourage them to think about their future careers, lifestyle choices, and what it takes to achieve those goals.

11. If You Were Given $500 Now, What Would You Do with It?

This hypothetical scenario can be a fun way to test their understanding of saving, spending, and investing.

Conclusion: An Investment in Their Future

As we reach the end of this enlightening journey, it's crucial to realize that teaching our children about money is not just a one-off lesson but a lifelong curriculum. Money is not merely a piece of paper or a number in a bank account; it's a tool that, when used wisely, can provide freedom, opportunities, and endless possibilities. The lessons contained in this guide are more than just tips or tricks; they are foundational principles that can make a significant impact on your children's future. Every conversation you have, every example you set, and every rule you teach is an investment in their financial future. There is no better gift than the gift of knowledge. So, let's make a pledge to set our kids on the path of financial wisdom because if we don't teach our children about money, then who will?

In this guide, we didn't just scratch the surface; we delved deep into the core principles that can help set your child on a path to financial freedom and responsibility. So, take these lessons to heart and let's prepare our kids for a financially sound future.

Introduction to "20 Rules for Entrepreneurs"

In the ever-evolving landscape of business, the role of an entrepreneur is both exciting and precarious. According to the Global Entrepreneurship Monitor, there are over 582 million entrepreneurs in the world. But here's a sobering fact: 90% of startups fail, according to a report by Failory. So, what separates the successful entrepreneurs from those who fall by the wayside? Well, it's not just luck or timing; it's also about adhering to certain principles that provide a firm foundation for success. The "20 Rules for Entrepreneurs" you're about to delve into are a distillation of these principles. Each rule is backed by empirical data, personal anecdotes, and a touch of emotional wisdom to help you connect, understand, and implement them in your entrepreneurial journey.

1- If You Screw Up, Don't Dwell on It. Learn and Move On

Mistakes are the stepping stones to success. A study published in the Harvard Business Review revealed that failure-tolerant leaders, those who treat mistakes as learning opportunities, tend to run more innovative and collaborative companies. When you stumble, pick yourself up, analyse what went wrong, and use that knowledge to avoid similar pitfalls in the future.

2- Constantly Read Biographies of Other Entrepreneurs

Bill Gates reads 50 books a year. Warren Buffet spends 80% of his day reading. The lives and journeys of other entrepreneurs are treasure troves of wisdom and inspiration. By diving into their stories, you not only learn what to do but also what not to do, offering you a well-rounded education that's hard to find elsewhere.

3- Manage Anxiety and Your Imagination

Anxiety is an entrepreneur's constant companion, but it's how you manage it that counts. According to the American Psychological Association, moderate stress can actually improve performance and productivity. The key is to channel your anxiety into constructive paths, like problem-solving and strategic planning.

4- Join an Advisory Group

Never underestimate the power of collective wisdom. According to the Harvard Business Review, CEOs who utilize external networks produce higher firm growth and customer satisfaction rates. An advisory group of seasoned entrepreneurs can offer invaluable insights and mentorship.

5- Anticipate Recessions and Tough Times

Forewarned is forearmed. Goldman Sachs reports that the U.S. has experienced an economic recession every 10 years since the end of World War II. By planning for downturns, you'll be in a better position to weather financial storms.

6- Distribution is everything

No matter how great your product is, if it doesn't reach the customer, it's worthless. A report by CB Insights found that 17% of start-ups fail due to poor distribution. Focus on a robust sales and distribution strategy.

7- Win the Right People Over

Employees are your greatest asset. According to a Gallup study, highly engaged teams show 21% greater profitability than those who aren't engaged. Winning the right talent can make or break your startup.

8- Stay in Creation Mode

Innovation is the lifeblood of entrepreneurship. Companies that innovate generate 67% more in sales, according to a PwC report. Always be in the mindset of creating something new or improving existing products.

9- Sweat Everything

Details matter. A study from the University of Notre Dame found that CEOs who are detail-oriented are 33% more likely to get top performance ratings. From finances to customer service, leave no stone unturned.

10- Be Patiently Aggressive

In entrepreneurship, timing is everything. A study by Startup Genome found that timing contributes to 42% of the difference between success and failure. Be aggressive in your goals but patient in your approach.

11- Focus on the Vision When Things Get Hard

When the journey gets tough, it's easy to lose sight of your end goals. According to a study by Leadership-IQ, 76% of employees say they have a clear understanding of their company's vision. Make sure you and your team always focus on the bigger picture.

12- Identify Your Blue Ocean Strategy

In a saturated market, uniqueness is the key. The book "Blue Ocean Strategy" recommends creating new market spaces rather than competing in overcrowded industries. Find your unique value proposition.

13- Don't Waste Your Money on PR Firms

Public relations don't have to be expensive. A Nielsen study found that 83% of people trust recommendations from friends and family over traditional advertising. Use your network for effective, low-cost PR.

14- Celebrate Histories Fast

Victories, no matter how small, deserve recognition. A study by Deloitte found that recognizing achievements can lead to a 14% increase in employee engagement. Celebrate your wins, but remember, time is of the essence.

15- Your Word Matters 10x More When You're Small

Trust is the foundation of any successful business. The 2019 Edelman Trust Barometer report found that 67% of consumers say they'll buy first from a company they trust. Be honest and transparent in all dealings.

16- Ask for Help

No one is an island, especially in business. Don't hesitate to seek help when you need it. According to a survey by UPS, 70% of small businesses that receive mentoring survive for five years or more.

17- Network Daily

Your network is your net worth. A study by LinkedIn found that 85% of all jobs are filled through networking. Make it a daily habit to reach out, connect, and cultivate relationships.

18- Keep Recruiting

Talent is the fuel that drives the engine of your business. According to a report by McKinsey, top-performing talent is up to eight times more productive. Always be on the lookout for potential team members.

19- Teach Everyone on Your Team How to Negotiate

Negotiation skills are vital in every aspect of business. A study by Harvard Law School found that negotiation training delivers a return on investment of up to 50%. Equip your team with this invaluable skill.

20- Luck is Part of the Game

While hard work and strategy are essential, sometimes luck plays a part. A study published in the journal "Management Science" found that luck and timing do play significant roles in a company's success. The harder you work, the luckier you get.

Conclusion: The Entrepreneurial Blueprint

Entrepreneurship is a complex, challenging, and incredibly rewarding journey. These 20 rules are your roadmap, drawn from extensive research, factual data, and emotional intelligence. They are designed to help you navigate the often-turbulent waters of business ownership. Implement them, and you'll be well on your way to joining the ranks of the successful 10% of entrepreneurs.

Introduction to "Art of Conversations"

In a world bustling with fleeting connections, the art of conversation stands as a testament to the depth of human relationships. This chapter delves into the vibrant heart of dialogue, offering a kaleidoscope of ways to spark genuine connections. Just as the Indian bazaar is alive with a symphony of sights, sounds, and colours, these 50 pathways to conversation promise a rich tapestry of interpersonal exchange.

1. Initiate with a Greeting

Dare to be the one who breaks the ice with a warm "hello," much like the first rays of sunlight dispelling the morning's chill.

2. Make Introductions Count

When you meet someone, make your introduction memorable, like a unique signature on a canvas.

3. Embrace the Risk of Engagement

Step into conversations with the boldness of a pioneer, expecting fruitful outcomes as a farmer anticipates a bountiful harvest.

4. Keep Your Sense of Humour Handy

Laughter is the universal language of connection, so share your light-hearted side as freely as a musician share melodies.

5. Practice Varied Conversation Starters

Like a chef experimenting with recipes, try out different conversational openers to see which ones bring the best response.

6. Make Names Your Mantra

Value people by remembering their names; it's as personal as a tailor-made garment.

7. If You Forget, Ask Again

Should a name slip your mind, show respect by asking once more, just as one would politely request a second helping of a delightful dish.

8. Show Genuine Curiosity

Let your interest in others shine as brightly as your curiosity about a new city you're exploring.

9. Share Your Story

Don't wait to be asked; share your narrative as openly as a book invites readers to its pages.

10. Reflect Their Words

Mirror what others say to show you're listening, like an echo in the mountains that validates the cry of the traveller.

11. Communicate with Zest

Talk about your passions with enthusiasm, which can be as contagious as the energy at a festival.

12. Be a Social Explorer

Venture out to meet new people as eagerly as an adventurer sets off on a journey to uncharted lands.

13. Honour Individuality

Respect others' unique views as you would appreciate a diverse garden of flowers, each with its own beauty.

14. Be Authentically You

Allow your true self to shine through in conversations, offering the comfort of authenticity, like home-cooked food offers solace to the soul.

15. Have Your Elevator Pitch Ready

Be able to succinctly describe your work or passion, just as a poet captures vast emotions in a few lines.

16. Reintroduce Yourself When Needed

If someone may not recall your name, reintroduce yourself, ensuring your identity is as clear as the morning sky.

17. Share Something Intriguing

Keep a captivating fact or story about your work ready, as a spice that adds an unexpected but delightful flavour.

18. Read Body Language

Be aware of nonverbal cues, both yours and others', as a musician is aware of the silence between notes.

19. Engage with Openness

Greet others with a smile and eye contact, as inviting as the aroma of freshly brewed chai.

20. Regularly Acknowledge Acquaintances

Recognize those you see often, making each acknowledgment as refreshing as a cool breeze on a warm day.

21. Seek Shared Interests

Find common ground in conversations, just as roots seek water to nourish the growth of a new relationship.

22. Offer Help Generously

Lend assistance where you can, sharing your abilities as freely as a tree offers its shade.

23. Let Others Be Experts

Encourage people to share their expertise, giving them the stage like a soloist in a symphony.

24. Engage in Ritual Questions

Partake in routine social inquiries, using them as stepping stones to deeper dialogue, much like a gentle stream leading to a river.

25. Show Enthusiasm for Their Interests

Celebrate what others love, as one would rejoice in the success of a dear friend.

26. Balance Sharing and Receiving

Ensure that the conversation is a two-way street, mirroring the give-and-take of the tides.

27. Be a Well-Rounded Speaker

Speak on a variety of subjects, offering versatility in conversation as a bazaar offers in goods.

28. Stay Informed

Keep abreast of current events to discuss relevant topics with the ease of a local discussing the weather.

29. Share Your Emotions

Express your feelings and beliefs openly, as a musician pours his soul into his song.

30. Use "I" Statements

When sharing personal experiences, speak from your perspective to offer authenticity as a signature on a painting.

31. Show Visual Interest

Let your body language convey your interest in the conversation, as vibrant as the colours in a festival

32. Extend Invitations

Invite others to join you in activities and events. It's akin to opening the doors to your home, offering a space for new memories and shared experiences.

33. Maintain Connections

Find creative ways to stay in touch with those you meet. It's like tending a garden, ensuring that the seeds of friendship you plant today can blossom into enduring relationships tomorrow.

34. Value Opinions

Actively seek and respect others' viewpoints. It's like exploring a library filled with diverse genres, each offering unique insights and knowledge.

35. Look for the Positive

In every encounter, search for the good in people. Approach interactions like a treasure hunt, looking for gems of virtue and goodness.

36. Personalize Your Farewells and Greetings

Start and end your interactions with a personal touch, using their name and a warm gesture. It's the human equivalent of bookmarking a page in a favourite book, marking the moments of connection for both of you.

37. Be Social and Collegial

Take time to foster warmth and friendliness with neighbours and colleagues. It's the daily weaving of social fabric that turns a community into a place of belonging.

38. Express Interest in Deepening Ties

Let people know you value them and desire to strengthen your connection, much like nurturing a budding friendship into a lifelong bond.

39. Follow Up on Past Conversations

Asking about topics discussed previously shows that you cherish and reflect on your interactions, like savouring the taste of a good meal long after it's finished.

40. Listen for Clues

Pay attention to the details in people's speech. It's often the little things that reveal the most about their desires and concerns, similar to how a small spice can change the flavour of a dish.

41. Ask Open-Ended Questions

Questions that cannot be answered with a simple 'yes' or 'no' open the door to richer dialogue, inviting stories and reflections as colourful and varied as a market bazaar.

42. Know When to Change the Topic

Just as a musician senses when to change the rhythm, you should feel when a conversation needs a new direction to maintain its flow.

43. Discover Passion Points

Find out what excites and motivates the other person. Their passions can illuminate the conversation like fireworks in a Diwali sky.

44. Offer Compliments

Genuine praise can warm hearts and build confidence, acting as a catalyst for stronger connections.

45. Send out Positive Signals

Encourage others to engage with you by being approachable and open, much like a home with its doors flung open to welcome guests.

46. Seek Out Enjoyable Company

Make an effort to spend time with people whose company you enjoy, just as one would revisit a favourite spot by the river to feel peace.

47. Simplify Your Stories

When sharing experiences, start with the essence, then embellish as interest dictates, much like painting the outline of a scene before adding intricate details.

48. Include Everyone

In group settings, be inclusive in conversation, sharing the joy of interaction as one would share food at a communal table.

49. Watch for Non-Interest Cues

Be attentive to signs of disengagement and be ready to steer the conversation to more engaging waters, akin to adjusting the sails on a boat for a smoother journey.

50. Prepare for Social Engagements

Before attending any event, think about potential conversation topics. This preparation can make social interactions as satisfying as a well-cooked meal after a day of fasting.

Conclusion: The Art of Conversation:

In conclusion, the art of conversation is like the very essence of life's dance – it requires rhythm, sensitivity, and a genuine desire to engage. By mastering these 50 ways to initiate and maintain conversations, you welcome the world into your personal narrative, creating a mosaic of relationships that enrich your life and the lives of others. Embrace each interaction as an opportunity to learn, share, and connect, and watch as the tapestry of your social fabric becomes as diverse and vibrant as the streets of India itself.

"Simple Wealth: Everyday Lessons from Millionaire Homes"

Introduction

"Simple Wealth: Everyday Lessons from Millionaire Homes" is your personal guide to understanding the basics of smart money management, inspired by the practices of the wealthy. This book is crafted to be as simple as a chat with a wise elder, filled with straightforward insights and practical advice. It's designed for anyone who wishes to turn their financial situation around, whether you're starting from scratch or looking to enhance your existing knowledge.

Breaking Down Wealth Lessons

- Assets and Liabilities - The Building Blocks of Wealth: Imagine your finances as a game of balance. Assets are like the fruits from a tree you plant, growing and giving more over time. Liabilities, in contrast, are like a leaky bucket, constantly draining what you have. We'll explore how to grow your garden of assets while patching up those leaks.

- Hard Work Beats Inheritance: Just like winning a race by your own sweat and effort, wealthy parents teach their kids that true success comes from their own hard work, not just family money. This section emphasizes the value of personal drive and achievement.

- Money - A Force for Good: Money, often seen as the root of all evil, is actually a powerful ally. It's like a tool in your kit — when used wisely, it can build wonders. We'll shift the perspective on money from something to fear to something to wisely wield.

- Financial Literacy - The Key to Freedom: Learning about money should be as basic as learning to cook a simple meal. This chapter makes financial concepts digestible, teaching you how to manage and grow your wealth effectively.
- Networking - Building Valuable Connections: Think of networking as sowing seeds in different fields. Some will grow into fruitful opportunities. This part focuses on how to build and maintain relationships that can open doors to success.
- Good Debt vs. Bad Debt: Like a wise farmer who knows when to borrow water to nurture his crops (good debt) and when borrowing would lead to loss (bad debt), this section teaches the art of using debt as a tool for growth, not a path to financial stress.
- The 80/20 Rule - The Secret to Efficiency: Picture your efforts as seeds. Some will grow abundantly with little effort. This principle teaches you to focus on actions that yield the most significant results, a strategy favoured by the wealthy.
- Problem-Solving Equals Wealth: Like a craftsman who gets paid for every problem he fixes, this chapter illustrates how solving problems can be a lucrative path, encouraging innovative thinking.
- Investing in Self - The Ultimate Asset: This part advocates for self-development as the most profitable

investment, stressing the importance of constantly enhancing your skills and knowledge.

- The Real Face of Money: Like a magnifying glass that reveals the true nature of what's underneath, money amplifies your true self. This section discusses using wealth responsibly and ethically.
- Patience in Wealth Building: Building wealth is compared to nurturing a tree; it requires time, patience, and consistent care. This chapter stresses the importance of long-term planning over quick fixes.
- Raising Income, Not Just Cutting Back: This section contrasts the effects of growing your income versus merely reducing expenses, emphasizing the importance of expanding your financial inflow.
- Passive Income - Earning While You Sleep: Like setting up a shop that makes money even when you're not there, this chapter explores ways to create income streams that don't require your constant attention.

Conclusion

"Simple Wealth: Everyday Lessons from Millionaire Homes" is a guide that simplifies the journey to financial well-being. It's a collection of timeless wisdom presented in a relatable and easy-to-understand manner, tailored for anyone who aspires to a life of financial security and freedom. This book is your companion in transforming your financial understanding and setting the stage for a prosperous future.